Backyard Bird Watchers

A Bird Watcher's Guide to

GOLDFINCHES

By

Shalini Saxena

Gareth Stevens
PUBLISHING

Please visit our website, www.garethstevens.com. For a free color catalog of all our high-quality books, call toll free 1-800-542-2595 or fax 1-877-542-2596.

Cataloging-in-Publication Data

Saxena, Shalini.
A bird watcher's guide to goldfinches / by Shalini Saxena.
p. cm. — (Backyard bird watchers)
Includes index.
ISBN 978-1-4824-3903-8 (pbk.)
ISBN 978-1-4824-3904-5 (6-pack)
ISBN 978-1-4824-3905-2 (library binding)
1. Goldfinches — Juvenile literature. 2. Bird watching — Juvenile literature. I. Saxena, Shalini, 1982-. II. Title.
QL696.P246 S29 2016
598.8'85—d23

First Edition

Published in 2016 by
Gareth Stevens Publishing
111 East 14th Street, Suite 349
New York, NY 10003

Copyright © 2016 Gareth Stevens Publishing

Designer: Laura Bowen
Editor: Therese Shea

Photo credits: Cover, p. 1 (goldfinch) Danita Delimont/Gallo Images/Getty Images; cover, pp. 1–32 (paper texture) javarman/Shutterstock.com; cover, pp. 1–32 (footprints) pio3/Shutterstock.com; pp. 4–29 (note paper) totallyPic.com/Shutterstock.com; pp. 4–29 (photo frame, tape) mtkang/Shutterstock.com; p. 5 Lonnie Gorsline/Shutterstock.com; p. 7 (drawings) nuconcept/Shutterstock.com; p. 7 (left photo) D and D Photo Sudbury/Shutterstock.com; p. 7 (right photo) gregg williams/Shutterstock.com; p. 9 (canary) John A. Anderson/Shutterstock.com; p. 9 (goldfinch) StevenRussellSmithPhotos/Shutterstock.com; p. 12 Jack Nevitt/Shutterstock.com; p. 13 Bobby Dailey/Shutterstock.com; p. 14 Steve & Dave Maslowski/Science Source/Getty Images; p. 15 Anatoliy Lukich/Shutterstock.com; p. 17 (main) Helen E. Grose/Shutterstock.com; p. 17 (thistle) Nancy Bauer/Shutterstock.com; p. 17 (coneflower) Milosz_M/Shutterstock.com; pp. 19, 20 rck_953/Shutterstock.com; p. 21 Gerald Marella/Shutterstock.com; p. 23 Gary Meszaros/Science Source/Getty Images; p. 25 Anthony Mercieca/Science Source/Getty Images; p. 27 Vishnevskiy Vasily/Shutterstock.com; p. 29 topten22photo/Shutterstock.com.

Printed in the United States of America

CPSIA compliance information: Batch #CW16GS: For further information contact Gareth Stevens, New York, New York at 1-800-542-2595.

CONTENTS

Words in the glossary appear in **bold** type the first time they are used in the text.

MY NEW BIRD FEEDER

Things I Want to See

- ☐ goldfinch feathers up close
- ☐ the types of things a goldfinch eats
- ☐ a goldfinch nest
- ☐ a goldfinch egg
- ☐ a baby goldfinch!

4

Living in my neighborhood is great. I get to see so many different kinds of birds in my own backyard! I especially love goldfinches because I can see them year round, even in the winter.

Mom and Dad helped me hang a bird feeder in our backyard, which I can see from my room. I hope it brings more goldfinches here. I'm going to use this **journal** to help keep track of their habits. I can't wait to start bird-watching!

The bird feeder is already working! Where I live, in the northeastern United States, American goldfinches can be found all year.

A BACKYARD TREASURE

8

You can guess what color many goldfinches are by their name: they're yellow, like gold! But I've also seen some that are olive green and light yellow. My **field guide** tells me these are probably the females. It's spring now, so males are a very bright yellow and have a black spot on their forehead.

In winter, males look more like the females. That's because they **molt** in the summer. Both males and females have black and white feathers on their wings and tail.

My field guide has pictures like these. It helps me pick out which birds are goldfinches.

male

female

male

female

7

CANARY COUSINS

The yellow feathers are a good start, but there are other things that help me spot goldfinches:

- short, pointed beaks
- short tails that are **notched**
- bodies usually no longer than 5 inches (13 cm)

The first time I saw a goldfinch, I thought it might be a canary because of its color. It turns out that both goldfinches and canaries are in the finch family. That's why they have a lot in common. Finches usually have brightly colored feathers. They're also songbirds, which means they have special calls.

Unlike canaries, goldfinches aren't pets. American goldfinches are sometimes called "wild canaries." I can't get too close to goldfinches without scaring them away. I use **binoculars** to watch them.

canary

goldfinch

It's easy to tell goldfinches and canaries apart. Goldfinches usually have some black feathers on their wings and tail.

A WORLDWIDE BIRD

The American goldfinch is the state bird of:

New Jersey
Washington
Iowa

When I visited my cousins in Washington state last week, I saw two types of goldfinches in their backyard. At home, I usually see just American goldfinches, which are found all over North America. But from the northwestern part of the United States to Peru, the lesser goldfinch is common, too. Both types look alike, but we had fun trying to tell them apart!

There are two other types of goldfinches. Lawrence's goldfinches are found in California, Arizona, and Mexico. European goldfinches are in Europe, Asia, and Australia.

range map of American goldfinch

North America

- year round
- summer
- winter

The American goldfinch stays in some places all year. In other places, you can only find them during certain seasons.

GOLDFINCH GRUB

Weird!
Goldfinches can eat upside down.

sunflowers

My bird feeder has been a big success! I read that goldfinches will sometimes eat bugs, but they're mostly granivorous. That word just means they eat seeds. In nature, flowers with seeds provide food for goldfinches. That's why they love sunflowers.

I usually put nyjer seeds in the feeder. These look like black rice. I mix some sunflower seeds in there, too. Our net feeder has many small openings. Birds with larger beaks can't take any food. It also allows many goldfinches to feed at once.

Feeders that allow goldfinches to hang upside down also keep away birds that can only eat right-side up.

13

FRIENDLY FLIERS

Tip: My parents help me clean my bird feeders and the ground below them every 2 weeks or so. This keeps the birds healthy.

Goldfinch flocks, also called charms, can be large. Yesterday, I counted 30 birds! I read that goldfinches usually feed in groups. Goldfinches in some parts of North America **migrate** for certain seasons. They usually travel in flocks for this, too.

Something funny I noticed is that the goldfinches don't seem to mind sharing seeds with birds like pine siskins and other finches. These birds are often part of goldfinch flocks. I wanted to make sure the birds don't fight for food, so I hung up a few more feeders.

goldfinch

pine siskin

This pine siskin is sharing a feeder with a goldfinch.

A GOLDFINCH GARDEN

Watch Out!

A goldfinch could be lunch for snakes, hawks, squirrels, or cats! Even birds like blue jays might want to eat goldfinch eggs.

Dad helped me find some websites with tips on bringing more goldfinches to the yard. We planted some sunflowers and coneflowers because goldfinches love their seeds. We're going to get some thistle and milkweed, too, but we have to be careful. Some plant types can harm other plants. Goldfinches use thistle and milkweed for food and nests.

I also read that goldfinches like water. I saved my allowance to buy a birdbath for the yard. The goldfinches love it. It's so cute when they splash around!

thistle

coneflower

Goldfinches may use feeders less in the winter, but they still enjoy birdbaths.

MAKING MUSIC

Goldfinches are as fun to listen to as they are to watch! When they fly, I can hear them calling "po-ta-to-chip" or "per-chick-o-ree." These calls help birds in a group know where the others are. The males sometimes sing longer songs, too.

Yesterday, I saw a hawk swoop down near the feeders. I think it was trying to eat a goldfinch! But the goldfinches started making a "ch-ween" sound to warn of danger, and the hawk went away.

Bird Calls:

contact calls = how birds in a flock tell others where they are

alarm calls = how birds warn others of danger

begging calls = how baby birds ask for something

flight calls = how birds tell others where they are while flying

Goldfinches can continue to learn different songs and calls throughout their life.

19

PAIRING UP

Today, I heard a male goldfinch calling "tee-yee!" to a female. It's almost summer now, which is when goldfinches start looking for **mates**. That must be his mating call! Then he started singing and chasing her through the air.

The female began zigzagging in the air as the male flew straight behind her. Then they both flew in a circle over and over. How funny! During the mating season, many males try to win over one female.

Wow!
Goldfinches in a pair usually have the exact same flight call.

This is the pair I saw earlier. I wonder if the female has found her mate!

SETTLING DOWN

Goldfinch Nest Materials:

- thistle
- milkweed
- pieces of dead trees, weeds, and vines
- grass
- caterpillar webs and spider silk

Goldfinches build nests in thick bushes and trees in late summer. They usually choose to live in open spaces like farms, fields—or our backyard! I saw a nest in one of our trees. Last week, I saw a female bringing weeds to the tree. She must have used those to create the nest. I read that goldfinches use caterpillar webs and spider silk to hold the nest together. The nest can even hold water!

Using binoculars, I saw the nest was cup-shaped. It had five light blue eggs in it!

It takes about 6 days for goldfinches to build their nest. Goldfinch mothers usually lay between two and seven eggs.

GROWING GOLDFINCHES

The female goldfinch sat on the eggs for about 2 weeks while the male fed her. The eggs finally **hatched** yesterday. The baby goldfinches were born with no feathers and closed eyes. I see both parents feeding their **nestlings**. They chew seeds first and then give them to the babies. I'm glad my parents didn't feed me like that!

Baby goldfinches open their eyes after 7 days. Soon after, they're ready to leave the nest. I'm going to watch them as much as I can before that.

The father goldfinch feeds his young by putting chewed seeds into their mouth.

FAST-LEARNING FLEDGLINGS

What's Next?

After her fledglings leave the nest, a female goldfinch may find another mate and lay more eggs. They usually don't have more than two **broods** a year.

Goldfinch **fledglings** learn so fast! Yesterday, they couldn't even leave the nest or feed themselves. When I saw them earlier today, though, they were already hopping around on branches. They were learning how to leave the nest. I heard the mother calling nearby. I think she was helping them.

Later in the day, the fledglings were flying! One landed on our roof. Fledglings may stay close to their parents for a couple more days. However, by 10 to 16 days old, they're ready for the world!

Goldfinch fledglings already have all their feathers by the time they leave the nest. Their colors change after their first winter.

27

FUN FOR ALL

I've had so much fun bird-watching that I decided to join a bird-watching club with other kids my age. I share stories about goldfinches and hear about the birds they're watching. We're even going to take trips around the state to see different bird types!

The club is a great way to learn about **ornithology** (or-nuh-THAH-luh-jee). I can't wait to learn more about birds and bird-watching. In the meantime, I'll watch the goldfinches in my yard!

Birds Online!

I'll ask Mom and Dad to help me set up a **webcam** so I can see everything that happens at the feeders when I'm gone.

GLOSSARY

binoculars: handheld lenses that make objects seem closer

brood: a group of young birds that were all born at the same time

field guide: a book that helps someone identify birds, plants, animals, rocks, or other things in nature

fledgling: a young bird that has grown feathers and is learning to fly

hatch: to break out of an egg

journal: a book in which one writes down what happens to them or their thoughts

mate: one of two animals that come together to make babies

migrate: to move from one area to another for feeding or having babies

molt: to lose feathers or outer coats in order to grow new ones

nestling: a young bird that isn't able to fly away from the nest yet

notched: having a cut shaped like the letter V

ornithology: the study of birds

webcam: a small video camera that is used to show live images on a website

FOR MORE INFORMATION

Books

Alderfer, Jonathan. *National Geographic Kids Bird Guide of North America.* Washington, DC: National Geographic, 2013.

Cate, Annette LeBlanc. *Look Up! Bird-Watching in Your Own Backyard.* Somerville, MA: Candlewick Press, 2013.

Websites

American Goldfinch
theiwrc.org/kids/Facts/Birds/goldfinch.htm
Learn about the habits of the American goldfinch on this site.

Birding with Children
www.birdwatching.com/tips/kids_birding.html
Check out this site to get bird-watching tips and learn what you need to start.

How to Attract Goldfinches
birding.about.com/od/Specific-Birds/a/How-To-Attract-Goldfinches.htm
This site explains what you can do to bring more goldfinches to your backyard.

INDEX